H A B I T A T S

RIVERS AND LAKES

DAVID CUMMING

Wayland

HABITATS

Coasts	Mountains
Deserts	Polar Regions
Forests	Rivers and Lakes
Grasslands	Seas and Oceans
Islands	Wetlands

Cover: The Niagara river thunders over the huge Horseshoe Falls between the USA and Canada.

Contents page: Otters swim in the lakes and rivers of many countries all over the world.

Series and book editor: Rosemary Ashley
Series designer: Malcolm Walker

First published in 1995 by
Wayland (Publishers) Limited
61 Western Road, Hove
East Sussex, BN3 1JD, England

British Library Cataloguing in Publication Data
Cumming, David
  Rivers and Lakes. - (Habitats series)
  I. Title II. Bull, Peter III. Yates, John IV. Series
  574.5263

ISBN 0-7502-1490-2

Typeset by Kudos Editorial and Design Services, England
Printed and bound in Italy by L.E.G.O. S.p.A., Vicenza

CONTENTS

1. THE HYDROLOGICAL CYCLE

Water is essential for the survival of plants and animals. It makes up over 90 per cent of all plants and 70 per cent of all animals. All the biological processes which make life possible need water. Water is especially important for humans. Not only do we need it for drinking, we use it every day in our homes for cooking and washing, in our factories for manufacturing goods, and on our farms for growing food. We also use water for transporting goods and to make electricity.

More than half of the earth (about 66 per cent) is covered with water, nearly all of which (97.4 per cent) is salt water in the seas and oceans. About 2.5 per cent is frozen (in the Arctic, Antarctic and in mountain glaciers) and in the ground as groundwater. The remaining 0.1 per cent of water occurs in rivers and lakes, in the soil, in animals and plants, and in the air (as water vapour). The circulation of the earth's water (the hydrological cycle) constantly transfers water between all the places where it is stored. It is a huge, natural recycling system that keeps the earth's water supply in balance, for it ensures that as much water falls on the planet as is removed from it by evaporation.

Today, humans require more water than ever for all their needs. To provide this extra water, they have interfered with the hydrological cycle and disturbed the natural balance – for instance, by building dams. Humans do not want water to hinder their progress, so they have tried to tame rivers to prevent them flooding.

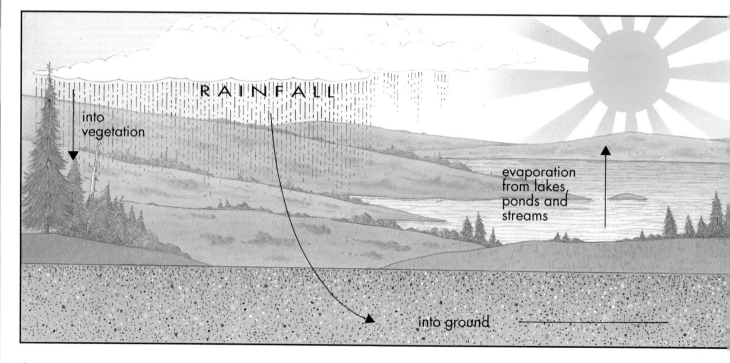

RAINFALL

into vegetation

evaporation from lakes, ponds and streams

into ground

Storm clouds bringing rain to top up the waters of Loch Sunart in Scotland.

This meddling with nature has usually created as many problems as it has solved, and the end result has often left us with less water rather than more. Some people now believe that we should change our ways to live in balance with nature, instead of trying to change nature to fit in with our lives.

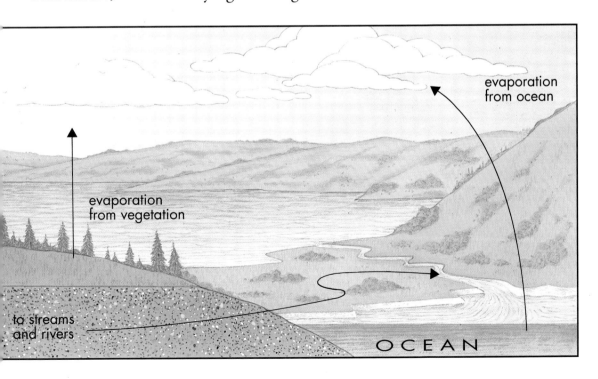

evaporation from ocean

evaporation from vegetation

to streams and rivers

OCEAN

This diagram shows how the earth's water is constantly recycled, in a process known as the hydrological cycle.

2. A RIVER'S ROUTE

A river is a large amount of water that flows downhill through a channel or a valley. Rivers are pulled downwards by the force of gravity, which is the reason why a river never flows upwards but always down. Because the oceans are lower than the land, most rivers flow down into them. Some rivers flow straight into oceans; others, called tributaries, enter the ocean by joining another, larger, river. A few rivers never reach the ocean, ending up in a lake or even disappearing into a marsh.

This map indicates the world's major rivers.

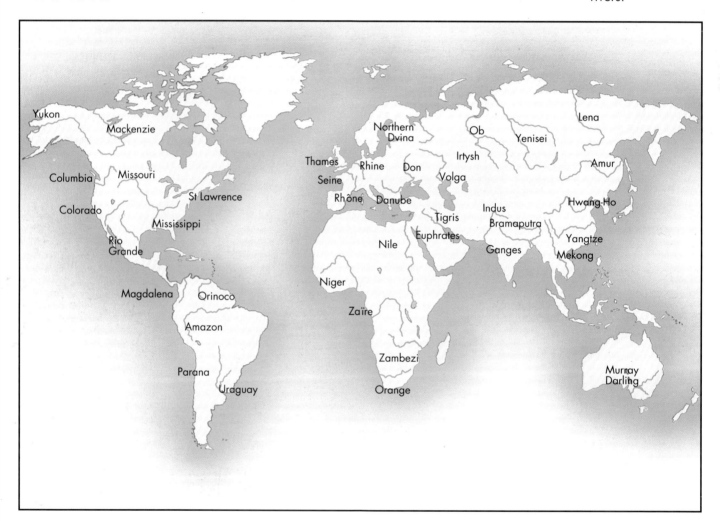

The source

Winds pick up water vapour in the air as they blow over the seas and oceans of the world. Most of the water vapour eventually falls as rain on the land. The rainwater seeps into the gaps and cracks in the soil and underground rocks. When these are full, the water bubbles out on the surface and trickles downhill; the trickle turning into a stream, the stream into a river.

Left The tiny River Rhine, near its source high up in the Swiss Alps.

The start of a river is called its 'source', and the place where the water bubbles up is the 'spring'. But not all rivers have a spring as their source: their water may be provided by melting glaciers. Many rivers have several sources, so geographers usually consider the river's true source to be the one furthest from the sea.

The character of a river changes greatly on the journey from its source to the sea. The landscape, too, alters along a river's route because a river has the power both to create and to destroy land.

The power of rivers

The power of a river depends on the amount of water in it and the steepness of the slope down which it is being pulled by gravity. Both affect how fast it flows. The most powerful rivers are ones full of water rushing down a steep slope.

However, a mountain stream also has a lot of power, even though it contains little water. Equally, a river flowing over gently sloping land can become very powerful after it has been swollen by heavy rain.

The more powerful the river, the more destructive it is and the more quickly it erodes (wears away) the land. Also, the greater its power,

Below Rivers are most powerful near their source. This is the young River Llugwy in North Wales.

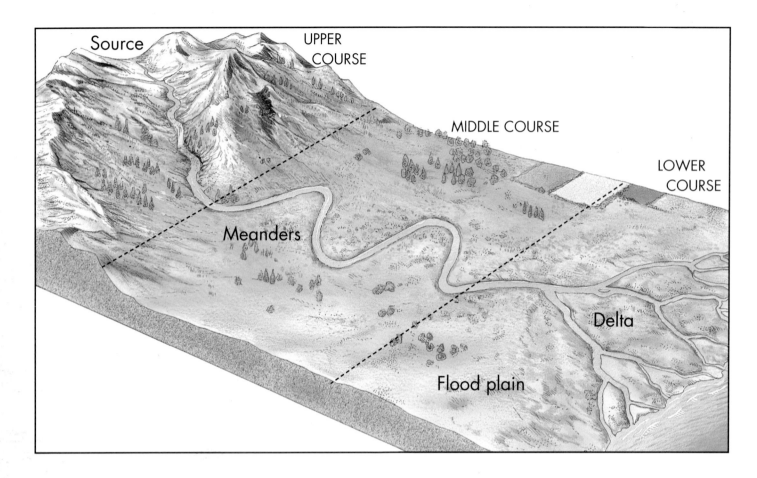

Source UPPER COURSE

MIDDLE COURSE

LOWER COURSE

Meanders

Delta

Flood plain

the more eroded land it can carry in its water. Thus, rivers can alter the shape of the land: land eaten away upriver can be transported and dropped downriver, forming new land. All the earth, sand, mud, stone and bits of rock transported by a river is called sediment. On its journey downriver, the sediment is ground up into fine particles, called alluvium. When the river floods, alluvium is spread over the land and provides fertile soil for farming, because it contains all the nutrients plants need to grow.

Above A river's journey from source to sea.

Below The V-shaped valley dug by the River Yellowstone in the USA.

The upper course

A river's route, or its course, can be split into three stages: upper, middle and lower. Near its source, a river is small but powerful because it is flowing fast downhill. It uses its power to erode downwards, often digging itself a deep, steep-sided, V-shaped valley.

Waterfalls and rapids are common sights in the upper course. Often, the river comes to a band of hard rock, on the other side of which the rock

Below In its middle course, a river's sideways erosion creates meanders (bends), like these on a river in Alaska.

is softer. The soft rock is worn away more quickly than the hard rock, so a ledge is left, over which the river tumbles as a waterfall.

Rapids are stretches of rough, fast-flowing water caused by layers of hard rocks in the river-bed. Softer rocks between them are worn away more quickly than the hard rock, forming steps, like mini-waterfalls. As it pours over the steps, the water gathers speed, crashing into and swirling around rocks in its bed.

The middle course

As the river flows on to the plains at the foot of the highlands, it loses power because it is no longer dropping steeply. The land on the plains is almost flat, with only a gentle slope towards the sea, so the current slows and the

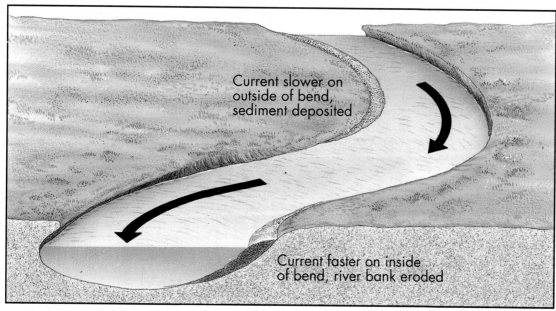

Current slower on outside of bend, sediment deposited

Current faster on inside of bend, river bank eroded

Left This diagram shows how a river erodes land.

river becomes weaker. Now, instead of eroding downwards, it begins to erode sideways, eating into its banks as it meanders, or winds, along its valley. The sideways action widens the valley – the river is like a huge wriggling snake, meandering left and right as well as down its length.

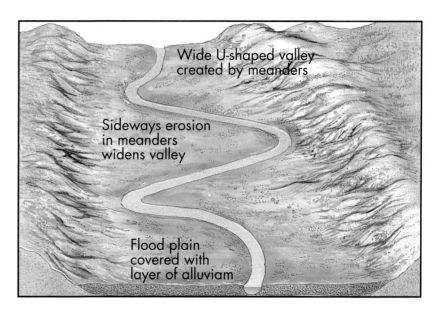

Wide U-shaped valley created by meanders

Sideways erosion in meanders widens valley

Flood plain covered with layer of alluviam

The current is fast on the outside of a meander (bend) and slow on the inside. So the outer bank is eroded away, while the inner bank builds up with material dropped by the slow-flowing water. As the outer bank crumbles (sometimes to leave a cliff), the inner one grows. This can result in a U-shaped bend as the river loops back on itself. Often the current wears away

The flood plain is the land lying alongside a river, which is regularly flooded.

Marshy islands in the Okavango delta.

An inland delta

The River Okavango, in western Africa, never reaches the sea. Starting in the hills of Angola, it flows through Namibia into Botswana. Here, the river fans out into many channels which flood in the spring, spreading 700,000 tonnes of sediment to create the world's largest inland delta. About 95 per cent of the water evaporates; the other 5 per cent turns into marsh between the delta's many islands. The islands are rich in wildlife, including zebras, elephants, hippos, crocodiles, lions, herons, pelicans, eagles and ducks.

the land inside the bend, straightening the river. Sediment fills each end of the bend and it is cut off from the river, forming a horseshoe shaped lake called an ox-bow.

As the river's meanders eat away the sides of the valley, flat land forms next to the river. This is called the flood plain, because when the river is full it will burst its banks and drown the land. The flood plain is covered with alluvium dropped by flood water, so it is good for farming. When a river floods, the largest materials in the water are released first, building up to form the river banks running alongside. Alluvium is carried a greater distance because it is made up of tiny particles.

The lower course

After zigzagging across its flood plain, the river enters the sea. A narrow opening is called a mouth, a wide one an estuary. By now the river's banks have eroded so much that the river valley has widened until it is hardly a valley at all. The river has lost all its power, after flowing across virtually flat land, and it stops meandering because it is too slow-moving to erode its banks. The river now flows too slowly to carry materials, so it begins to drop them, forming mud flats and sand banks.

A large river can block up its estuary with all the material it deposits. The material builds up into low, flat land and the river is forced to carve channels through it to reach the sea. This area is called a delta. Two rivers with large and constantly changing deltas are the Mississippi in the USA and the Ganges in India.

Fishing in a channel of the River Danube's delta. River deltas are a rich source of fish.

3. TYPES OF LAKES

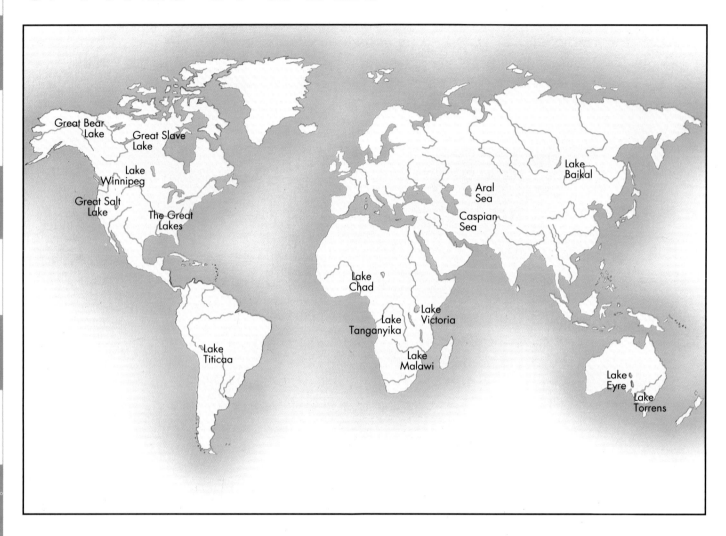

Great Bear Lake
Great Slave Lake
Lake Winnipeg
Great Salt Lake
The Great Lakes
Lake Titicaa
Lake Chad
Lake Tanganyika
Lake Victoria
Lake Malawi
Aral Sea
Caspian Sea
Lake Baikal
Lake Eyre
Lake Torrens

This map indicates the location of the world's largest lakes.

A lake is an area of water completely surrounded by land. Unlike rivers, which contain moving water, lakes contain still water. In fact, lake water does move, but much more slowly than river water. Most lakes have a river that enters and leaves, so water flows through the lake, in one end and out the other. Water also circulates within a lake, especially near its surface, where the sun's rays heat up the water. The warmth makes the top layer of water heavier than the cold water underneath, so the warmer water sinks and the colder water rises, and the process is repeated constantly.

Lakes come in all shapes and sizes. Some are so big that they are considered to be inland seas,

The largest lakes
The world's ten largest lakes are:
Caspian Sea, central Asia . . . . .*(371,000 sq km)*
Lake Superior, North America . .*(83,270 sq km)*
Lake Victoria, Africa . . . .*(68,800 sq km)*
Lake Huron, North America . . . .*(60,700 sq km)*
Lake Michigan, North America .*(58,020 sq km)*
Aral Sea, central Asia . . . .*(50,000 sq km)*
Lake Tanganyika, Africa . . . . . .*(32,900 sq km)*
Great Bear Lake, North America .*(31,790 sq km)*
Lake Baikal, Russia . . . .*(30,500 sq km)*
Lake Malawi, Africa . . . .*(22,490 sq km)*

like the Caspian Sea and the Aral Sea in southern Russia, or the enormous Great Lakes in North America and Lake Victoria in East Africa.

Freshwater and saltwater lakes

Most of the water entering a lake is brought by rivers and streams. The lake water is topped up by rain draining off the nearby land. River and stream water contains minerals from the rocks over which it has travelled, and rainwater carries chemicals picked up in the air. The flow of water through a lake keeps it 'fresh' and this movement prevents large amounts of chemicals and minerals from building up, so plants and fish can survive in the water without harm.

Below Few creatures or plants can live in the salty Dead Sea.

If water does not flow out of a lake, then the minerals and chemicals are trapped. The sun's heat evaporates the water, leaving increasing amounts of chemicals and minerals in the lake, especially salt. The water in the lake may turn from fresh water to salt water. The Dead Sea, between Israel and Jordan, for example, is nine times more salty than the oceans. As its name suggests, little can live there.

In very hot climates, the sun can evaporate all the water in a lake, leaving only salt. The Great Salt Lake in Utah, USA, is a salt lake, as its name implies. Lake Eyre – Australia's largest lake – usually has a layer of salt up to 4.5 m thick, in place of water.

Left Lake Nagadi, in the Great Rift Valley in Africa, was formed as a result of a fault in the earth's crust.

Disappearing lakes

All lakes will eventually dry up because they fill with sediment brought by the rivers and streams entering them. A lake can also 'die' if a river stops supplying it with water or if the river's flow is altered so that the lake starts to receive less water than it loses through evaporation.

A lake can also drain away if its rim is worn down by a river leaving it. A worn-away rim will allow a greater amount of water to flow out. If more water now leaves the lake than enters it, the water level will drop, perhaps to the point where the lake dries out.

Natural lakes

Most lakes form in deep hollows in the ground. In North America, Asia and Europe, many of these hollows were gouged out by glaciers during the last Ice Age, about 18,000 years ago. When temperatures rose, at the end of the Ice Age, the glaciers melted. They left behind huge mounds of boulders and rocks, called terminal moraines, which had been scraped off the land. The moraines often blocked the ends of valleys, allowing water to build up

Below Wast Water, in Britain's Lake District, formed in hollows which had been scraped out by a glacier.

behind them, creating lakes like those in the Lake District of northern England. Small lakes often form in the hollows in the moraine itself.

There are also lakes in places where faults, or cracks, in the earth's crust have caused a long section of land to sink. The cracks are usually parallel, so they create long, thin lakes. The best examples of lakes formed in this way are to be found in the Great Rift Valley, in Africa, which extends northwards through East Africa to Lebanon, in the eastern Mediterranean. At its southern end are Lakes Malawi and Tanganyika, and at the northern end, the Dead Sea. The Dead Sea formed on land which had slipped 400 m below sea level, so it is the lowest lake in the world.

Lake Baikal, in eastern Russia, is the world's deepest lake (up to 1,741 m) because it formed in a huge crack in the earth's crust.

Water near the surface of Lake Baikal freezes in winter.

The oldest lake
Most lakes have filled up with sediment by the time they are a million years old. The exception is Lake Baikal, in Russia. This lake is so deep that it will take a very long time to fill up with sediment. Lake Baikal formed 25 million years ago, when a 9-km-deep crack appeared in the Earth's crust. Rain and river water then began draining into the crack, bringing sediment with it. Today, the greatest depth in Lake Baikal is just under 2 km, which means that 7 km of sediment has settled on the bottom of the original crack. If it has taken 25 million years for that amount of sediment to build up, Lake Baikal will continue to exist for at least another seven million years.

As its name suggests, Crater Lake in Oregon, USA, is a lake in the top of an old volcano.

Sometimes a lake is formed by rainwater filling up the crater of an extinct volcano. A good example of this type of lake is Crater Lake in the state of Oregon, USA.

Underground lakes are found in limestone areas. Limestone is a 'soft' rock which is easily dissolved by rain. Rainwater trickles through holes and cracks,

Measuring lakes

Which is bigger: a shallow lake which covers a large area of land (surface area) or a deep lake which is very small? The freshwater lake with the largest surface area is Lake Superior, one of the Great Lakes of North America. Yet the freshwater lake containing the most water is Lake Baikal, which has a much smaller surface area – 30,500 sq km compared to Lake Superior's 83,270 sq km. The reason for this is that Lake Baikal is extremely deep, at one point reaching 1,741 m. In fact, there is as much water in Lake Baikal as in all the Great Lakes put together: it holds 20 per cent of all the earth's fresh water. The Caspian Sea, which is a saltwater lake, is the largest lake in the world, both in terms of its surface area and the amount of water in it. The Caspian Sea has a surface area of 371,000 sq km and reaches depths of 1,000 m.

Ice forming on Lake Superior in winter.

eating its way into the rock. Sometimes, the water reaches a layer of hard rock beneath the limestone which prevents it going any further. Here it collects and over thousands of years it can hollow out a cave with a lake in it. Alternatively, the rain can flow along the top of the layer of hard rock, tunnelling through the limestone as an underground river.

Artificial lakes

Not all lakes have been formed by nature; some have been created by humans. The most common artificial lake is the one caused by a dam across a river. The river's water builds up behind the dam, flooding the land and forming a lake, called a reservoir. The lake is usually for storing water for nearby cities or for a hydroelectric power station – frequently for both purposes. The largest reservoir in the world is Lake Volta, in Ghana. It has a surface area of 8,480 sq km and a length of 400 km. However, the reservoir that holds the most water is at Bratsk, on the River Angara in eastern Russia.

In the Netherlands, in northern Europe, artificial lakes, called polders, have been created behind dams along the coast. The land in the Netherlands is very low, so it is easily flooded by the sea. The dams prevent this happening. They have been built across estuaries and the entrance to bays. The water in the polders used to be salty, but with the sea kept out and rivers constantly feeding them, it is becoming fresh water.

Small artificial lakes form in gravel pits when rainwater collects in the hole left after the gravel has been removed.

A reservoir created by a dam across the River Tumut, in the Snowy Mountains of Australia. The reservoir supplies a nearby hydroelectric power station.

4. RIVERS AND WILDLIFE

Salmon are strong enough to leap over rapids and to swim against fast-flowing water.

The upper course

Only animals and plants that have adapted to living in fast-flowing water can survive in a river's upper course. Since most rivers start in mountainous regions, the water is cold. Nevertheless, the clear, rushing torrent is an ideal habitat for wildlife, for it is also clean and full of bubbles of oxygen, created by the swirling current.

Plants, like water starwort and water crowfoot, have developed long roots to secure them in the stony river bed, together with flexible stems which bend rather than break in the strong current.

Limpets and snails use their suckers to attach themselves to rocks and stones. The riffle beetle, or water penny, has a wedge-shaped, rough-edged shell which it uses for jamming itself into cracks to stop it from being swept away.

The streamlined shape of trout and salmon allows them to battle against the water's flow. Both these species of fish are very powerful for their size, particularly the salmon, which easily leaps up over obstacles such as rapids and weirs.

Otters can often be seen among the thick vegetation beside a river in its middle course.

The middle course

As the current slows down, sediment is released. This drops to the river bed to form a thick muddy layer, full of nutrients, in which plants can flourish.

These plants are vital to the survival of wildlife in and alongside the river, and animals and fish – from the tiny to the very large – feed on them. Beneath the water surface small fish and insects shelter among their roots and stems.

Above the water reeds, rushes and other tall plants provide excellent cover and nesting places for birds and small mammals.

The smallest plants in a river are microscopic algae, which provide food for insects and fishes. They are invisible except when the water contains so many

Huge water lilies growing on the River Amazon in South America.

of them that it turns into a green scum. The largest river plant is the giant water lily, seen on the River Amazon. Its leaves can grow to over 2 m across and they are strong enough to take the weight of a child.

The biggest river animal is the hippopotamus. It can measure over 4 m long and weigh 4 tonnes. Hippos are found only in Africa, where they feed on the grasses on the river banks.

The most dangerous river creatures are the carnivorous piranha fish of South America and the crocodiles and alligators to be found in the lakes and rivers of hot countries.

The lower course
Most of the wildlife seen in the the middle course is even more plentiful further downriver, where the current is slower. However, in estuaries and

Hippos are amphibians, able to live in water as well as on land. But they prefer to spend most of their lives in water, which keeps them cool.

deltas there is less variety, because many freshwater plants and animals cannot live in the salty seawater pushed in by the tides. Worms and crustaceans have grown accustomed to the salt and happily inhabit the mud banks where the river meets the sea. They provide food for passing flocks of birds.

In hot countries, mangrove forests grow at the mouths of many rivers. The biggest mangrove forest is the Sunderbans, on the Ganges delta in India and Bangladesh. At high tide, the trees are half underwater and have developed two sorts of roots to survive. Long roots hang down from the mangrove trunks to hold them upright and to prevent them being swept away. Small tube-like roots poke up through the mud to take in oxygen when the tide is out.

Long roots prevent this mangrove bush from being washed away by the tide.

The strangest river animal
The odd-looking duck-billed platypus lives only in the rivers of eastern Australia. It closes its eyes and ears when it swims underwater, so it has to rely on its sense of touch to scoop up insects, worms and shellfish with the bill (beak) after which it was named. The platypus measures up to 50 cm in length and is a mammal which hatches its young from eggs. In the past, so many of them were killed for their fur that the species was in danger of being wiped out, but now that it has been declared illegal to hunt the platypus, their future is more secure.

5. LAKES AND WILDLIFE

Reeds and grasses growing in the marshy land bordering a lake in Canada.

A lake provides a very rich and varied wildlife habitat. It is also a good example of an ecosystem, a self-contained world in which all the plants and animals depend on each other for their survival: removing or damaging one of them can set off a chain of events which can affect all their lives.

Animal adaptors

Many species of wildlife have developed special features or lifestyles to allow them to survive in a lake habitat. The water spider, for example, is the only spider to live underwater. It spins itself a silk cocoon beneath some floating weeds. Then it goes to the surface to trap bubbles of air between the hairs on its body and legs. The spider releases the air inside the cocoon, enabling it to live there. It only leaves its underwater home to collect more air bubbles and to hunt for insects.

As its name implies, the lilytrotter (or jacana) bird can walk across floating plants. It can do this because it has 8-cm-long, thin toes, which spread its weight evenly over the leaves.

Right A water spider's underwater home.

Left A black-throated diver, or loon, at the edge of one of Canada's many lakes.

Below A kingfisher diving into a river to catch a small fish.

Beetle power

In the 1960s a fast-growing, floating weed from Brazil found its way into Lake Moondarra, Australia. By the early 1970s the water was covered with a green carpet of weed which was starving the lake of oxygen and endangering the lives of the creatures that live there. Australian scientists decided that the safest and quickest solution was to import a species of Brazilian beetle which eats the weed. Within two years, the beetles had cleared the weed from the lake and all was well.

The long toes of the lilytrotter (or jacana) enable it to walk on floating river plants.

The land beside a lake is usually marshy. Rushes, reeds, marsh marigolds and irises flourish here, along with trees that like damp soil – for example, willow and alder. Arrowhead and water lilies grow in the shallow water around the lake's edge. Their roots are in the mud on the lake-bed, but their leaves and flowers either protrude into the air or float on the water. Further out from

Baikal seals basking in the summer sun.

Life in Lake Baikal

Freshwater Lake Baikal is a unique habitat. Until modern times, it was undisturbed by humans because of its isolated location in the wilderness of Siberia, eastern Russia. As a result, it is home to some 1,200 species of animals and 500 species of plants, most of which are found nowhere else. Scientists are also convinced that yet more species exist, undiscovered, in its dark depths.

The Baikal seal is the only freshwater seal in the world. Its ancestors were trapped in the lake when rivers linking it with the Arctic Ocean dried up thousands of years ago. There are fewer than 100,000 Baikal seals now because they have been hunted by the local people for their fur and meat.

East Africa's soda lakes

Many of the Great Rift Valley lakes in eastern Africa are full of a mineral called soda, or sodium carbonate. There is so much soda in the water that only algae and a species of small shrimps can live in them. Millions of flamingoes flock to the lakes to feed off the shrimps and algae. The birds sieve the harmful water through their beaks, separating the algae and shrimps from it. The algae contain a red-coloured dye which gives the flamingoes their pink colour. The flamingoes breed at Lake Natron where the water is so unpleasant that they need not fear other animals stealing the eggs from their nests.

The lake water evaporates in the hot climate to leave a layer of soda on the lake bed. Kenya exports thousands of tonnes of soda every year for the manufacture of glass, soap and washing powders.

Flamingoes feeding in the soda-filled waters of Lake Nakuru, Kenya.

the shore there are submerged plants, like water milfoils and waterweeds. They, too, have their roots in the mud, but unlike floating plants, they grow underwater. Free-floating plants, like duckweed, water-soldier and bladderwort, can be seen in deep water. Their roots are not attached to the bottom and they float on or just beneath the surface.

The roots of the marsh plants and trees help to prevent the shore of the lake slipping into the water, and they also provide shelter for birds and animals coming to drink or fish. As well as providing shelter and egg-laying places, the aquatic plants in the lake produce oxygen through photosynthesis, which dissolves in the water, allowing all the plants, fish and insects to breathe.

Leaves and flowers from the plants fall to the bottom of the lake and decay in the mud. Insect larvae, shellfish and worms live here and feed on the rotting material. They help to keep the water full of oxygen, because as the plant matter decays, the oxygen is absorbed.

The plants are eaten by insects, which are in turn eaten by fish which are eaten by birds – this is the lake's food chain put very simply. Removing one of the links in the chain puts other creatures in danger because they have nothing to feed on.

6. RIVERS AND FLOODS

Peple refer to 1993 as the year of the bad floods. Devastating floods along the River Mississippi in the summer were followed in the autumn by serious floods in Britain, Germany and France. It was said that all these floods were caused by the weather: an unusually high amount of rain had fallen in a very short time. Many people were not convinced by this explanation: they blamed human interference with nature.

River engineering

Valmeyer, Illinois, will soon be a ghost town, like several others drowned by the Mississippi in 1993. Its inhabitants are moving to a new Valmeyer, now being built on higher ground near by. The flood water not only swept away homes, it also swept away millions of dollars-worth of engineering work which had been carried out to tame the river.

The huge, winding Mississippi near Cairo in Illinois. In spite of all the engineering schemes for flood prevention, the river still floods the flat land on either side of its banks.

Two hundred years ago the Mississippi had a mind of its own. Naturally unpredictable and dangerous, the river shifted every year, eating away huge chunks of bank and flooding even larger areas of land. This was a nuisance to the newly industrializing USA, especially as much of the river was unnavigable. Late in the nineteenth century, it was decided to take the river out of nature's hands and to bring it under human control, so that it would help, not hinder, US development. Thus, one of the most ambitious river engineering schemes in history was begun.

So that barges could use the Mississippi, thousands of stone walls were built into the river. These caused the currents in the river to dig a 3-m deep channel along the river's length. To allow farms, towns and industries to be built on the flood plain, the river was walled in. High earth banks, or levees, were built along the banks to hold back flood waters. Dams, too, were built on the Mississippi's main tributaries, to regulate the amount of water entering the river. The Mississippi was also straightened by cutting through the land at the neck of large meanders. This improved the flow of water and made journeys quicker, for the river became 240 km shorter.

Above These brick walls have been built to stop the Mississippi pouring over the top of a levee.

It took a hundred years and $10 billion to tame the Mississippi. Every year $180 million is spent on maintaining all the alterations. After all this time and money, have humans triumphed over nature? Judging by the flood damage of 1993, the answer seems to be that they have not.

Critics of river engineering on the Mississippi argue that far from curing the flood problem, it has made it worse: less land may be flooded, but the floods are much deeper now, so the damage is greater. They say that because the Mississippi holds less water, it floods more easily.

Left The 1993 floods on the Mississippi and Missouri rivers were some of the worst this century. This flooded town is on the Missouri, near Chester, Illinois.

27

Nowadays, river engineers accept that a river has its own character, which is determined by its width, depth, slope and shape. Altering any one of these characteristics causes resistance from the river. For instance, shortening the Mississippi made it flow faster, so more sediment was eroded from upstream and deposited further down. Huge sand banks were created downriver and the river began to meander again, eventually adding 80 km back to its length.

Bangladesh's Flood Action Plan

These houses in Bangladesh have been built on stilts to prevent them being flooded by the River Ganges.

The consequences of engineering work on the Mississippi is worrying news for people living in Bangladesh. They are about to become 'guinea pigs' in a river-engineering plan which is much more ambitious than the Mississippi's.

The country of Bangladesh exists thanks to the two billion tonnes of sediment dumped every year on the coast of the Bay of Bengal by the Ganges, Brahmaputra and Meghna rivers. These three rivers have created the largest delta in the world, and Bangladesh occupies most of it.

The flat, low-lying land of Bangladesh floods easily. Every summer, after the heavy monsoon rains have filled the rivers, at least 20 per cent of the country is flooded; some years virtually all of it is underwater and life comes to a halt. It is one of the poorest countries in the world; most of the people are farmers and the floods often leave many of them with nothing.

Like the Mississippi, river engineers say it will take one hundred years to cure the floods. Like the Mississippi, too, the engineers plan to squeeze the

River Brahmaputra between concrete-filled levees to stop it from flooding and eroding precious farming land. Some 8,000 km of levees will also be built along the other rivers and channels in the delta. Opponents of this Flood Action Plan point to the levees constructed in the 1960s along the Brahmaputra. These need $20 million spent on them every year to stop them being eaten away by this giant river. They wonder how Bangladesh will be able to afford to look after thousands of kilometres of levees.

Bangladeshi river engineers reply that there is no option. In other countries people can move away from a river's flood plain. The people of Bangladesh do not have this choice because most of their country is on a flood plain. So many people live in this tiny country that there is no space in places free from flooding. The engineers say that if they do not stop the floods, there is no hope of improving life in Bangladesh. Unless the rivers can be controlled, Bangladeshis will always have to live with flooding. Just as the Mississippi once stood in the way of progress in the United States, so the Ganges, Brahmaputra and Meghna rivers are holding up development in Bangladesh.

Floods and human activity

Many geographers say that we have only ourselves to blame for floods. Flooding usually follows heavy rain because a river cannot hold all the rainwater draining into it. The land is like a huge sponge which soaks up rainwater. We have covered the land with so many roads and buildings that there is little left to absorb the rain. As a result much more water ends up in our rivers than before, so floods are more common and more serious. This problem was very evident in early 1995, when the River Rhine carried so much water that towns along most of its length were flooded. Much of the low-lying land near the Rhine's delta in the Netherlands, Belgium and northern France were under water.

Raised banks help to protect villages in the Ganges delta from floods.

7. WATER FOR DAILY LIFE

The demand for water

Since humans first walked on the earth, water has been essential for their survival. Therefore, the early civilizations all developed alongside large rivers: in Egypt by the Nile, in Mesopotamia (modern Iraq) by the Tigris and Euphrates, in Pakistan by the Indus, in China beside the Hwang-Ho (Yellow) and Yangtze rivers.

Over the centuries, changes in our daily lives have meant that we need more water, not less, in our homes and cities: dishwashers and washing machines, for example, require a lot of water, so do car washes and swimming pools. Industry, too, uses vast amounts of water.

A lake for life

In many of the poorer countries of the world, water can still play an important part in the survival of a community. South American Aymara Indians have been living in their floating homes on Lake Titicaca, between

The Cambodians use their local river for washing themselves and their clothes, and for water for their homes.

30

Bolivia and Peru, for nearly 2,000 years, safe from attackers. The lake is some 4,000 m up in the Andes Mountains, and is full of islands of totora reeds, which are strong enough to support a village of huts. The huts are made of the reeds, as are the boats which the Aymara Indians use for transport on the lake and the baskets and containers they make for sale. The lake also provides the Aymara with fish to eat and plants to feed their cattle, as well as water for drinking and washing.

The reeds growing on Lake Titicaca are used for making boats and island homes.

Hindu pilgrims bathing in the sacred waters of the River Ganges at Varanasi in India.

A holy river

The River Ganges in India is a sacred river for Hindus, the followers of Hinduism, the main religion in India. They believe that bathing in the Ganges will wash away their sins and bring them good luck. Hindus also believe that their souls will be saved after death if their ashes are spread on the river.

Many poor Indians cannot afford to have their dead relatives burnt, so their bodies are put directly into the river. To prevent the spread of disease, the Indian government is concentrating resources on cleaning up the Ganges, and has bred special flesh-eating turtles to dispose of the bodies. To stop people catching them to eat, the government has declared these turtles a protected species.

Water for pleasure

As well as being a necessity, water helps us to enjoy life. We use our lakes and rivers for all sorts of leisure activities, from fishing and swimming to sailing and water-skiing, or just for relaxing beside. In cold regions, such as the northern USA, Canada, Norway and Russia, thick ice forms on lakes and rivers in winter on which people skate. Many people enjoy spending their holidays beside a lake or travelling by boat down a river, relaxing or visiting the historical buildings on its banks.

Rivers and lakes, too, have been – and still are – sources of inspiration for painters, writers, photographers and film-makers.

Above Rowers on the River Thames at Henley, near London.

Right Rivers have inspired many artists. This painting of a regatta on the River Seine, in France, is by Claude Monet.

8. WATER FOR FARMING AND FISHING

Of course, humans need food as well as water to live. For this reason water has influenced the location and the development of settlements, because a nearby source of water has enabled crops to be grown.

It is often said that the country of Egypt is the 'gift of the River Nile', because the river turned infertile desert sand into rich farmland. The Nile was able to do this because every year it flooded, leaving a new layer of alluvium for farmers. The alluvium was full of nutrients so the farmers had no need of fertilizers to replace the goodness removed from the soil by plants. As well as providing fertile soil, the Nile supplied the farmers with water for their crops. The Nile is not unique in this respect: farmers on all flood plains doubly benefit from the nearby river.

Fertile farmland beside the banks of the River Nile in Egypt.

33

Rivers and lakes are particularly important to farmers in countries where there is little rain or where there is a long dry season. In much of India it is dry for seven or eight months of the year. During this time farmers need to make up for the lack of rain by irrigation – that is, pumping or diverting water from rivers into channels, which carry it to the fields.

Fish farming

There are many fish farms in developing countries, where fish is an important part of people's diets. The farmers dig ponds by the side of rivers or build enclosures in the water, in which fish can be bred for sale. In developed countries too, such as Scotland, Norway and Canada, fish farming is now big business in lakes and estuaries, with

As the Aral Sea dries up, ships are left high and dry.

A dried-up sea

Diverting river water to irrigate farmlands has caused one of the biggest of all environmental disasters of the twentieth century – the drying up of the Aral Sea, in Kazakhstan (part of the former Soviet Union). Since the 1960s the Aral Sea has shrunk by 40 per cent, revealing 28,000 sq km of land. The Aral Sea was fed by two large rivers, the Amu Darya and the Syr Darya. In the 1960s, the water from these rivers was removed by canals to irrigate millions of hectares of thirsty cotton, which was so valuable to the Soviets that they called it 'white gold'. It mattered more to them than the future of the Aral Sea. As more water evaporated from the Aral than flowed into it, the sea began drying up. As it shrinks, the Aral's water gets saltier. Within a few years the world will have another Dead Sea.

most of the fish raised on the farms being sold abroad. Salmon, trout and shellfish are the most popular species on these farms.

Fish farms have brought many advantages. Fish that were once costly have become cheaper to buy. The farms have brought employment opportunities to country areas where it is often difficult to find work. However, chemicals have to be used in the enclosures where the fish are kept, to keep them free of disease. These chemicals sometimes drift away from the fish farm and affect the wildlife near by, sometimes killing plants and other creatures.

Often fish are bred that are strangers to the area where the farm has been built. If some of these manage to escape, they can disturb the natural balance in a river or lake which has evolved over centuries. Species of foreign fish can also carry germs, which may kill local fish that have no immunity to them.

Greedy fish-eaters, such as otters, seals, ospreys and herons, steal the farms' fish and can end up being shot by the owners, furious at the damage they have caused. Thus the otter and osprey, which are already endangered species, can be threatened even more by the arrival of a fish farm on their territory.

Lake Victoria, where plans to increase the amount of fish have resulted in their numbers dropping even further.

Stranger in the lake
Fish from Lake Victoria, in eastern Africa, is the main source of protein for the peoples living around it. As their populations have grown, the number of fish in the lake has declined. To increase the fish levels, Nile perch was introduced into the lake, with disastrous consequences. The perch, which can weigh up to 100 kg, attacked and ate all the local fish. Instead of fish numbers increasing in Lake Victoria, they dropped further.

9. WATER FOR INDUSTRY AND POWER

Humans have been using the power of flowing water for hundreds of years. Early on, buildings had to be built right beside or above rivers so that power could be transferred to machinery by means of a waterwheel. Watermills were so named because water power was used, via a waterwheel, for milling (or grinding) wheat grain into flour.

Later, in the Middle Ages, waterwheels were adapted to drive hammers in riverside workshops where iron tools were made. After the Industrial Revolution, factories no longer had machines powered directly by water, but they continued to be built alongside rivers because their machinery was powered by steam.

Today, many industries are still situated by rivers and lakes because they require huge quantities of water in their manufacturing processes. For example, to make just one tonne of steel, 250,000 litres of water are needed.

Machines are now powered by electricity, so water remains an important indirect and direct source of energy. As an indirect source, water is converted into steam at nuclear power stations to turn the turbines which generate electricity. Water is also used to cool the nuclear reactor to prevent it getting too hot and cracking. For these reasons, the power stations are located near rivers and lakes.

Water from the River Seine, in France, is used in a power station to generate steam for electricity.

This is the Kariba Dam, on the borders of Zimbabwe and Zambia. The dam has caused the River Zambezi to form a huge lake. The power in the water released by the dam is used to generate electricity.

Hydroelectric power

Water is a direct source of electricity in many countries, because the power of falling water can be used to turn turbines. In mountainous areas, hydroelectric power stations can be built across fast-flowing rivers which tumble down the mountainsides. On flat land, dams have to be built to raise the water level so that it can fall a sufficient distance to produce the power to turn the turbines.

The Glen Canyon Dam across the Colorado River in the USA.

Dam problems

Dams are provoking arguments all over the world. Governments say they are needed for electricity, for providing drinking water and irrigation. They say that these benefits outweigh the damage done by dams when valleys are flooded by reservoirs, and towns and villages have to be moved to higher ground. Conservationists say that dams upset the hydrological cycle and a river's natural character, resulting in untold environmental damage. They say that dams do much more harm than good, so they should not be be built.

10. WATER FOR TRANSPORT

Before roads and railways, water was the main means of travel and communication. People preferred to use rivers and lakes because it was easier and safer than struggling overland, where, laden with belongings, they were easy prey for bands of robbers.

In early times, people crossed stretches of water with the help of inflated animal hides. Then they learned to stretch the hides over a wooden frame to make a coracle, ideal for short journeys and light enough to be carried by one person. With the development of metal tools, trees could be chopped down and the trunks hollowed out into canoes or tied together to form rafts which could travel long distances. These were fine for going downriver, but returning upstream was impossible if the current was strong. The solution was to use teams of horses or people to pull the rafts back home. The invention of steam and then diesel engines eventually made this unnecessary since they could be used to power boats both large and small.

However, there were other obstacles which made travel along rivers difficult. Some rivers plunged over perilous waterfalls, others were blocked by rapids and many became too shallow for boats in the dry season when rainfall was small and water levels low. Little could be done about the waterfalls, but the rapids and shallows could be avoided by building dams to raise the water level. Starting in the nineteenth century, dams have been built along many of the world's major rivers to improve navigation on them.

The Welland Canal, on the St Lawrence Seaway in Canada, links Lakes Ontario and Erie, by-passing Niagara Falls. Ocean-going ships can use the canal to reach the Great Lakes.

Water transport is best?
The main reason for the development of the inland waterways of Europe is that it is cheaper to transport low-value, bulky goods, like coal or gravel, by water rather than by road. Water transport is also a better way of using resources because barges use less fuel than lorries and cause less pollution and damage to the environment. Nevertheless, 85 per cent of freight in the European Community goes by road because lorries provide a more flexible door-to-door service. Barges can only go where the waterways take them.

Gravel is transported by barge on the River Rhine in Holland.

Today it is possible for barges to travel across Europe, from the North Sea to the Black Sea, and across Russia, from the Baltic Sea to both the Black Sea and the Caspian Sea.

Canals

It would not have been possible to cross Europe, Asia or North America by water without the assistance of canals – human-made waterways which can take short-cuts to avoid obstacles. Canals have locks at either end to ensure that their water level never varies. The locks can raise or lower barges, which means that canals can connect rivers, lakes or seas at different heights.

A canal links the Rhine and Danube rivers in Europe and a series of canals joins the River Volga, in Russia, to the Baltic Sea. Canals, too, link the main rivers of Europe to enable goods to be transferred between factories, river ports and Rotterdam and Hamburg, two of the world's biggest ports. In North America, the St Lawrence Seaway allows ocean-going ships to reach ports on the Great Lakes during the summer months. The Suez Canal (linking the Mediterranean Sea to the Red Sea) and the Panama Canal (connecting the Atlantic and Pacific Oceans) save journeys of thousands of kilometres by land.

A single powerful tug tows fleets of barges along the Mississippi.

11. WATER POLLUTION

Left For far too long, we have cared too little about what is dumped into rivers and lakes.

People have been polluting rivers and lakes ever since they began settling beside them. Rivers, especially, have been treated as if they were huge drains and everything has been thrown into them. Once, rivers and lakes were able to clean themselves naturally. Bacteria in their waters could break down the waste to make it harmless. But, over the centuries, as cities and industries have expanded, they have created too much waste for the bacteria to cope with, so river and lake water has become steadily dirtier. In addition to increased waste, industries have also begun dumping metals and chemicals in the water, and these cannot be made harmless by bacteria.

Below A new water-cleaning plant on the River Ganges in India.

Water-borne illnesses

The problem of dirty water was recognized as long ago as 1389, when England's King Richard I forbade the dumping of rubbish and human and animal sewage in rivers near towns and cities. Few people obeyed the law. Consequently, outbreaks of deadly infectious diseases, like cholera and typhoid, became common, because they were caused by people drinking water containing human or animal sewage.

These diseases have been stamped out in rich countries, where human waste is treated before it is released into rivers and lakes. Water for drinking is also treated after it is pumped out of rivers and lakes, before being piped to homes. However, in many poor countries, diseases like cholera and typhoid remain a danger. There are few water-treatment plants and most homes lack running water, a toilet and a bathroom, so people have to wash in and drink from rivers containing human and animal waste.

Acid rain

The fumes and gases given out by industries and motor vehicles turn rain into nitric and sulphuric acid. This falls on lakes, turning the water acidic and killing the wildlife. British industry creates the acid rain that falls on the lakes of Scandinavia. Already some 90,000 lakes in Sweden are too acidic for fish and plants; a further 35,000 are approaching a dangerous level. To reduce their acidity, helicopters drop lime into the lakes, which neutralizes the acid and allows life to return to them. A further cause for concern is the amount of pollution coming from out-of-date factories in the former Communist countries of Eastern Europe.

Waste from a copper mine has harmed the wildlife in this river in Spain.

Industrial pollution

Industry has done the greatest harm to the quality of water in rivers and lakes. Heavy metals, such as mercury, lead, zinc, cadmium and copper are frequently discharged from factories directly into the water. Tiny amounts of these can kill wildlife. Equally dangerous are the PCB (polychlorinated biphenyl), chemicals used to make plastic, paint and glue.

Lakes are more at risk than rivers from industrial pollution because the waste is not washed away, but gradually builds up to become very poisonous. Lake Baikal, in eastern Russia, has suffered greatly from the factories on its shores. It has been estimated that one paper-making factory alone has allowed 1.5 billion cubic metres of highly poisonous chemicals to drain into the lake. Some of Baikal's plants and animals are now under the threat of extinction, including a tiny shrimp that eats algae and bacteria which purifies the water. Only the water in the centre of the lake is now purified by the bacteria. Since many of these endangered species are unique to the lake, they will not only vanish from Lake Baikal but from the face of the earth.

On the other side of the globe, in the 1970s pollution reached such a high level in Lake Erie, one of the North American Great Lakes, that it was considered 'biologically dead'. Nothing could live in the lake; the industrial cities of Cleveland and Detroit had effectively killed it. The other Great Lakes were also damaged by pollution, but not to the same extent as Lake Erie. As in other countries, new laws were introduced which forced factories to reduce their waste and banned certain products from being emptied into the lake. As a result, Lake Erie has been brought back to life.

In rivers, waste is swept downstream by the current. By the time it reaches the sea, all the heavy metals and toxic chemicals have blended together to create a 'killer cocktail' which can knock out creatures as large as whales. Beluga or white whales feed in the mouth of the St Lawrence River, which joins the Great Lakes to the Atlantic Ocean. Dead belugas are being washed ashore regularly. The bodies contain large amounts of chemicals. Their threat to humans and wildlife is so great that they are classified as toxic waste requiring immediate disposal.

Above In the 1970s, Lake Erie, one of the Great Lakes, was so polluted that nothing could live in its waters.

Left Poisonous chemicals in the St Lawrence River are endangering the survival of beluga whales in the Atlantic Ocean.

Algae on a lake in Sweden. It has been formed by agricultural chemicals which have drained off the nearby fields, and cause eutrophication.

Agricultural pollution

Farms, too, are a major source of water pollution. The chemical fertilizers and pesticides used on crops drain off the fields into lakes and rivers. Fertilizers are full of phosphates and nitrates which can cause eutrophication in lakes – when the water becomes over-rich in nutrients. Since the chemicals are not flushed away in the still water, they boost the growth of algae. It 'blooms', forming a thick, green layer on the surface of the water. The bloom blocks sunlight entering the water, so plants die because they cannot photo-synthesize. As they decay, they use up all the oxygen, suffocating the fish. Many conservationists are now arguing for a return to organic farming, that is, traditional methods which do not use chemicals in fertilizers or pesticides.

Water hyacinths: killers or curers?

Once, the water hyacinth was considered a threat to rivers and lakes. It spreads quickly across the surface, cutting out the light and starving the water of oxygen. However, recent studies have discovered that the plant absorbs nitrates and phosphates from the water. This reduces eutrophication. Provided its growth can be controlled, the water hyacinth may be useful in the future for lowering pollution levels.

12. THE FUTURE

For some nations water is very precious because it is in short supply. As their populations grow, the lack of water becomes even more of a concern, to the point, perhaps, where conflict could occur between neighbouring countries, should they be unable to agree on sharing a river's water. In regions such as the Middle East, the population growth is among the fastest in the world. There are few rivers and rainfall is low. The major rivers flow through countries that have been arguing and fighting between themselves for years over land and religion. Could water be a further cause for conflict?

In countries where there is plenty of water, mini-wars of words are increasingly common as people argue with their governments to preserve lake and river habitats from damage. In France protestors have successfully prevented a dam being built across the River Loire which would have flooded a valley. In Hungary, too, the construction of a new dam on the River Danube has been halted after mass demonstrations took place to oppose the dam.

All over the world people are now realizing that rivers and lakes have an important role in planet Earth's future. After centuries of abusing them, river and lakes are being treated with more respect.

The clear waters of a river in Malawi, far from the pollution of cities or industry. Hopefully, in the future lakes and rivers all over the world will once more become clean and pleasant habitats.

Glossary

Algae   Simple plants that include seaweeds and the scum on ponds.

Alluvium   Good farming soil that has been left by a river's flood waters.

Bacteria   Microscopic plants or animals, some of which purify water; others cause diseases.

Carnivorous   Flesh-eating.

Conservationists   People who try to protect the environment from being harmed.

Coracle   A small boat made from animal hides stretched over a wicker frame.

Course   A river's route.

Crustacean   A member of a species of animals that has a shell, like crabs and shrimps.

Delta   Low, flat land at a river's mouth formed from sediment dropped by the river as it enters the sea.

Ecosystem   The chain of relationships between species of animals and plants living in one habitat.

Environment   The surroundings in which humans, animals and plants live.

Erode   To grind or wear down, or wear away. The eroding process is called erosion.

Eutrophication   The process by which pollution in a lake may cause the water to become over-rich in nutrients, so that algae grow quickly and reduce the oxygen supply.

Evaporation   The change that takes place when water changes from a liquid to a vapour.

Evolve   To develop gradually, over many years.

Fertilizer   A substance added to farming land to make it better for growing crops. There are chemical fertilizers and natural ones, like animal manure.

Groundwater   Water in the spaces and cracks in the soil and underground rocks.

Habitat   The place where a species of animal or plant lives naturally.

Hydroelectricity   Electricity generated by the power of falling water.

Hydrological cycle   The circulation of the earth's water, in which water evaporates from the sea into the atmosphere, where it condenses and falls as rain or snow; also called the water cycle.

Ice Age   A period in history when much of the earth was covered with ice.

Industrial Revolution   The transformation in the eighteenth and nineteenth centuries of countries in Western Europe and the United States into industrial nations.

Irrigation   Supplying farming land with water through canals, channels and pumps.

Lock   A section of a canal that can be closed off by gates so that boats can be raised or lowered by letting water in or out.

Meander   To take a winding route.

Navigable   A river or lake deep enough to be used by boats or ships.

Nutrients   Substances that help plants and animals to grow.

Pesticide   A chemical sprayed on farm crops to kill insects that eat them.

Photosynthesis   The process by which plants use sunlight to produce oxygen.

Pollution   Making water or the air dirty with gases or solid waste.

Rodent   An animal, like a rat, that has large front teeth for gnawing things.

Sediment   All the materials carried by a river's current.

Soviet Union   A former group of republics in Eastern Europe and Northern Asia controlled from Moscow. The Soviet Union broke up into separate states in 1991.

Species   A group of animals or plants that are very similar.

Waterway   A route on a river or canal that can be used by boats or ships.

Wildlife   Animals and plants in their habitats.

Books to Read and Further Information

Lake by Lionel Bender (Franklin Watts, 1989)
The Ganges Delta and Its People by David Cumming (Wayland, 1993)
River by Lionel Bender (Franklin Watts, 1988)
River by Brian Knapp (Atlantic Europe, 1992)
The World's Rivers series (Wayland, 1991-94)
Magazines, like the *National Geographic* and *Geographical,* often contain articles on rivers and lakes.

For further information about animals and their habitats that are under threat, contact the following environmental organizations:

Friends of the Earth (UK)
26–28 Islington Green
London N1 8XE

Friends of the Earth (USA)
1045 Sansome Street
San Francisco
California CA 94111

Greenpeace (UK)
30-31 Islington Street
London N1 7JQ

Greenpeace (Australia)
3310 Angas Street
Adelaide 5000

Greenpeace (Canada)
427 Bloor Street West
Toronto
Ontario

Greenpeace (New Zealand)
Private Bag
Wellesley Street
Auckland

World Wide Fund for Nature
Panda House
Weyside Park
Godalming
Surrey

Picture acknowledgements
Bruce Coleman /A.Compost 21 (top), /D.Green 23 (top); D.Cumming 29,31 (lower); Eye Ubiquitous / M.Reed cover, /K.Howard 4, /L.Fordyce 16 (top), /K.Mullineaux 22 (top), /L.Fordyce 26, 27 (top), /J.Holmes 30; Frank Lane Picture Agency /S.McCutcheon 9, /V.Wisniewski 18, /D.Hosking 20, /Silvestris 22 (lower), /E.& D.Hosking 42, /M.Withers 45; NHPA /D. Woodfall 7 (lower), /Michael Leach 8, /A.Bannister 14 (top), /J. Gifford 14 (lower), /J.Hartley 15, /S.Kraseman 16 (lower); 17, /R.Kirchner contents page, 19 (top), /D.Watts 21 (lower), /Silvestris 23 (lower), /N.J.Dennis 24 (top), /A.Bannister 34 (top), /J.Carmichael jr 38 (lower), /P.Johnson 43 (top), /G.Lacz (lower); Photri 27 (lower); Hutchison Library V.Ivleva 35 (top), 41 (top), 44 (top), Still Pictures /Bergerot 10, /M.Libersky 24 (lower), 34 (lower); Wayland Picture Library /D.Cumming 7 (top), 11, /J.Waterlow 19 (lower), /D.Cumming 28, /I.Lilly 32, /J.Waterlow 33, 37, /L.Fordyce 39 (lower), /D.Cumming 40 (top), /L.Fordyce 40 (lower), /D.Cumming 41 (lower), /J.Waterlow 44 (lower).
Maps and diagrams on pages 6,8,9,10,12 are by Peter Bull, and on page 4-5 by John Yates.

INDEX

Numbers in **bold** refer to photographs